The AIER Chart Book

By AIER Research Staff

AMERICAN INSTITUTE *for* ECONOMIC RESEARCH

Great Barrington, MA

The AIER Chart Book

Economic Bulletin, Vol. L No. 7 July 2010

Published by:
American Institute for Economic Research
Economic Bulletin
250 Division Street
PO Box 1000
Great Barrington, MA 01230
888-528-1216
info@aier.org
www.aier.org

Economic Bulletin (ISSN 0424–2769) (USPS 167–360) is published once a month at
Great Barrington, Massachusetts, by American Institute for Economic Research, a
scientific and educational organization with no stockholders, chartered under Chapter
180 of the General Laws of Massachusetts. Periodical postage paid at Great Barrington,
Massachusetts. Printed in the United States of America. Subscription: $59 per year.
POSTMASTER: Send address changes to *Economic Bulletin*, American Institute for
Economic Research, Great Barrington, Massachusetts 01230.

Book Design and Production: Jonathan Sylbert
Cover Design: Jessica Shiner

ISBN 13: 978-091361073-2

Printed in U.S.A.

Foreword

We are proud of our "visual display of quantitative information," to use Professor Edward R. Tufte's description of the process, especially when we look at the standards of presentation found elsewhere. Although matters do seem to be improving, we still see countless grossly misleading or pointless charts in the business and financial press. The most common of these involve the graphical presentation of relatively small data sets, the use of arithmetic scales for series that grow over time, and the use of two-dimensional figures or glyphs to represent one-dimensional data. The latter include such devices as stick figures or pictures of little bags of money. The problem with these is that a figure that is, say, twice as tall as another is four times as large. The relationship intended by the chart maker or perceived by the reader may then only be guessed.

When we prepare charts, our foremost criterion is data density. Graphical presentations are best used to present data that are too voluminous to provide within text or in a table. Thus, whenever space permits, we plot data series as far back as they are available. We also use logarithmic or ratio scales (on which equal *percentage* changes appear as equal distances) whenever appropriate. Exceptions to this practice include instances where a series contains negative values, a series is a ratio or proportion, and, occasionally, when the absolute value of a series is of interest. We also try to avoid grid lines, which continue to appear in the charts of many publications. These may have been needed to achieve accuracy when things were done by hand, but they only add clutter and confusion to computer-generated graphics. The vertical shaded bars in some charts indicate periods of economic recession in the United States, as identified by the National Bureau of Economic Research. Constant-dollar data have been deflated by the Consumer Price Index unless otherwise noted.

We often receive compliments on our graphical presentations as well as requests for copies of specific charts apart from our publications. We are pleased, therefore, to present this collection of AIER charts, which we hope our readers will find timely, useful, and informative. We invite comments and suggestions for future updates of this booklet.

Charles E. Murray
President

i

Contents

Government

Financial Indicators

Energy

Sources

Money, Prices, and Interest Rates

Purchasing Power of the Dollar

(1792 = 1.00)

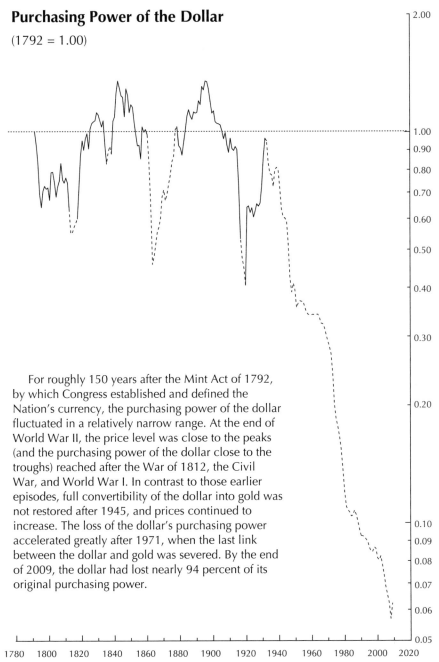

For roughly 150 years after the Mint Act of 1792, by which Congress established and defined the Nation's currency, the purchasing power of the dollar fluctuated in a relatively narrow range. At the end of World War II, the price level was close to the peaks (and the purchasing power of the dollar close to the troughs) reached after the War of 1812, the Civil War, and World War I. In contrast to those earlier episodes, full convertibility of the dollar into gold was not restored after 1945, and prices continued to increase. The loss of the dollar's purchasing power accelerated greatly after 1971, when the last link between the dollar and gold was severed. By the end of 2009, the dollar had lost nearly 94 percent of its original purchasing power.

Note: Purchasing power was calculated from the Wholesale Price Index (source: Bureau of Labor Statistics, U.S. Department of Labor). The broken portions of the curve are periods when redeemability of the dollar into the monetary commodities at fixed rates was suspended.

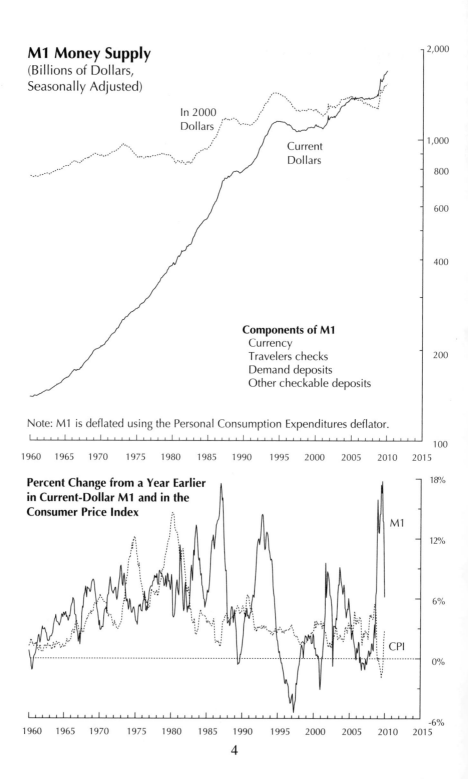

M1 Money Supply
(Billions of Dollars,
Seasonally Adjusted)

In 2000
Dollars

Current
Dollars

Components of M1
Currency
Travelers checks
Demand deposits
Other checkable deposits

2,000

1,000

800

600

400

200

Note: M1 is deflated using the Personal Consumption Expenditures deflator.

100

1960   1965   1970   1975   1980   1985   1990   1995   2000   2005   2010   2015

**Percent Change from a Year Earlier
in Current-Dollar M1 and in the
Consumer Price Index**

18%

M1

12%

6%

CPI

0%

-6%

1960   1965   1970   1975   1980   1985   1990   1995   2000   2005   2010   2015

4

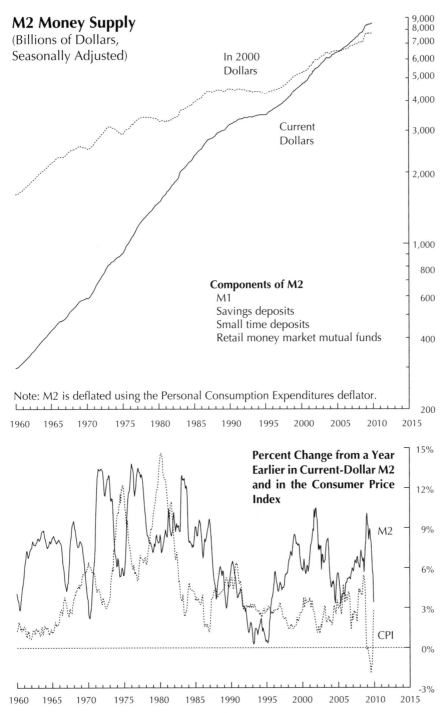

M2 Money Supply

(Billions of Dollars,
Seasonally Adjusted)

In 2000
Dollars

Current
Dollars

Components of M2
M1
Savings deposits
Small time deposits
Retail money market mutual funds

Note: M2 is deflated using the Personal Consumption Expenditures deflator.

9,000
8,000
7,000
6,000
5,000

4,000

3,000

2,000

1,000

800

600

400

200

1960   1965   1970   1975   1980   1985   1990   1995   2000   2005   2010   2015

Percent Change from a Year Earlier in Current-Dollar M2 and in the Consumer Price Index

M2

CPI

15%

12%

9%

6%

3%

0%

-3%

1960   1965   1970   1975   1980   1985   1990   1995   2000   2005   2010   2015

5

Indexes of Selected Foreign Exchange Rates

(Dollars Per Currency Unit, August 1971 = 100)

Note: After 1998 the exchange rates for marks, French francs, and lira are calculated from their conversion rates to the euro.

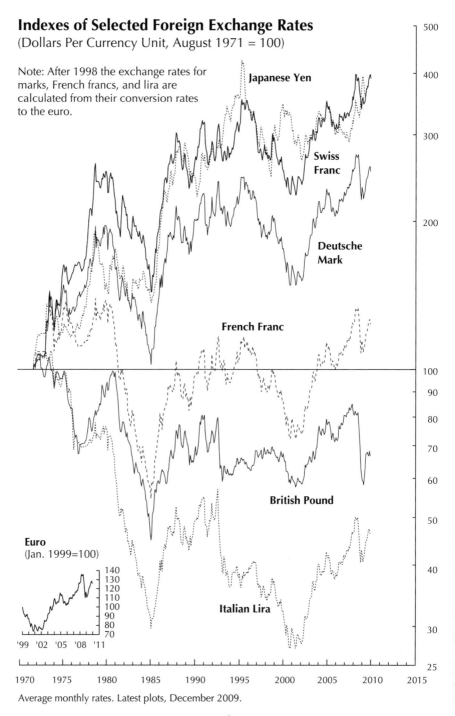

Japanese Yen

Swiss Franc

Deutsche Mark

French Franc

British Pound

Italian Lira

Euro
(Jan. 1999=100)

140
130
120
110
100
90
80
70

'99 '02 '05 '08 '11

1970   1975   1980   1985   1990   1995   2000   2005   2010   2015

500
400
300
200
100
90
80
70
60
50
40
30
25

Average monthly rates. Latest plots, December 2009.

6

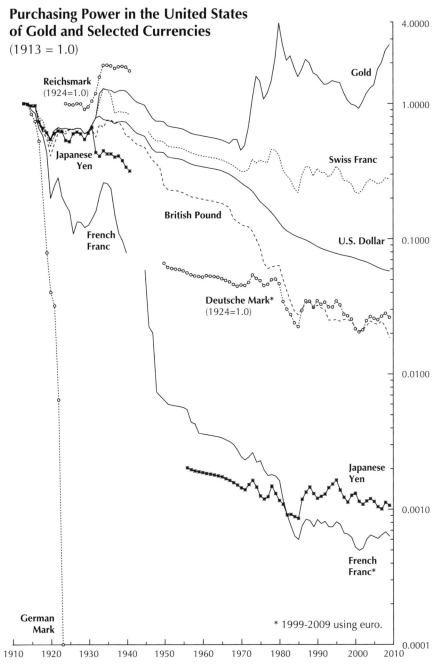

Purchasing Power in the United States of Gold and Selected Currencies
(1913 = 1.0)

Reichsmark
(1924=1.0)

Japanese
Yen

French
Franc

British Pound

Deutsche Mark*
(1924=1.0)

Gold

Swiss Franc

U.S. Dollar

Japanese
Yen

French
Franc*

German
Mark

* 1999-2009 using euro.

4.0000

1.0000

0.1000

0.0100

0.0010

0.0001

1910   1920   1930   1940   1950   1960   1970   1980   1990   2000   2010

Note: Purchasing power calculated from the implicit price deflator for U.S. GDP and the exchange rates of foreign currencies for U.S. dollars. Latest data, 2009.

7

Indexes of the Price of Gold in Selected Currencies (August 1971=100)

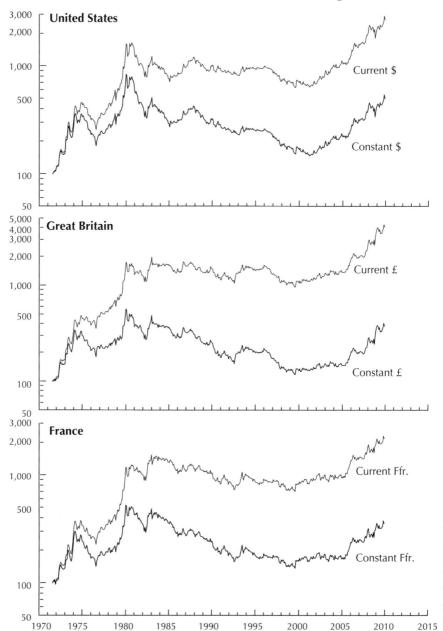

Note: The indexes of the price of gold in each country were calculated using as a base the prices into which each currency was officially convertible into gold immediately prior to the so-called Smithsonian Agreement of late 1971, and the subsequent end-of-month dollar price of gold and the exchange rate

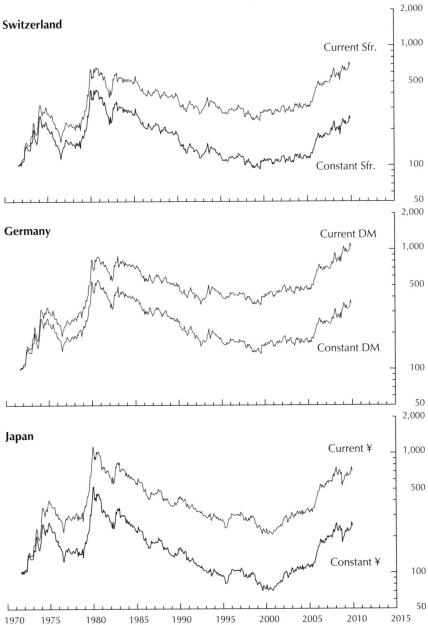

Switzerland

Current Sfr.

Constant Sfr.

Germany

Current DM

Constant DM

Japan

Current ¥

Constant ¥

for each currency against the dollar (using the euro for France and Germany after 1998). The indexes of the price of gold in terms of the purchasing power of each currency were calculated using each country's consumer price index (as published by the IMF) set to a base of 1971=100.

Latest plots: December 2009.

9

Purchasing Power of Gold

(1792 = 1.00)

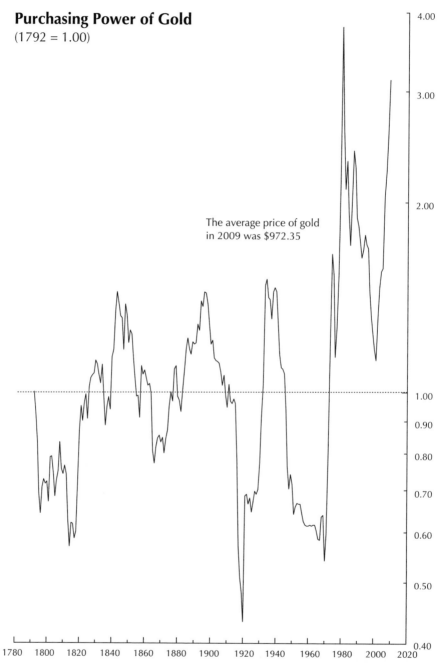

The average price of gold in 2009 was $972.35

Note: The changes in purchasing power shown in the chart were calculated from annual averages of the Wholesale Price Index (source: Bureau of Labor Statistics, U.S. Department of Labor) and the annual averages of the exchange ratio of dollars for gold.

Nominal and Real Yield on 10-Year Treasury Notes
(Percent)

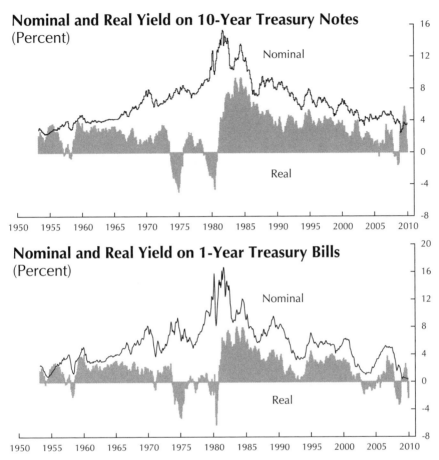

Nominal and Real Yield on 1-Year Treasury Bills
(Percent)

Note: Real yields calculated as the nominal yield minus the percent change in the Consumer Price Index over the previous 12 months.

Annual Average Bond Yield in the United States, 1798-2009

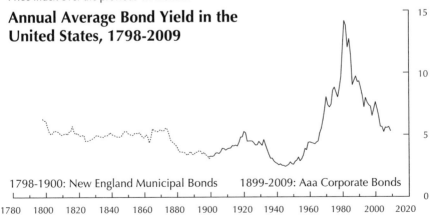

1798-1900: New England Municipal Bonds   1899-2009: Aaa Corporate Bonds

11

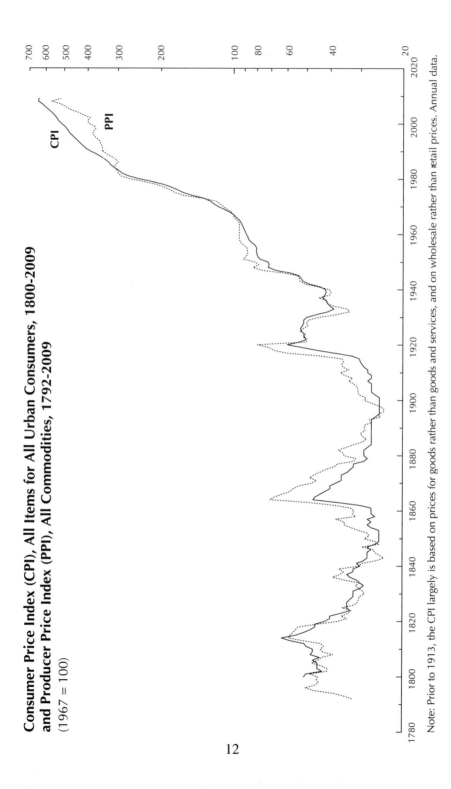

Consumer Price Index (CPI), All Items for All Urban Consumers, 1800-2009 and Producer Price Index (PPI), All Commodities, 1792-2009

(1967 = 100)

Note: Prior to 1913, the CPI largely is based on prices for goods rather than goods and services, and on wholesale rather than retail prices. Annual data.

12

Selected Components of the
Consumer Price Index, 1978-2009
(1978 = 100)

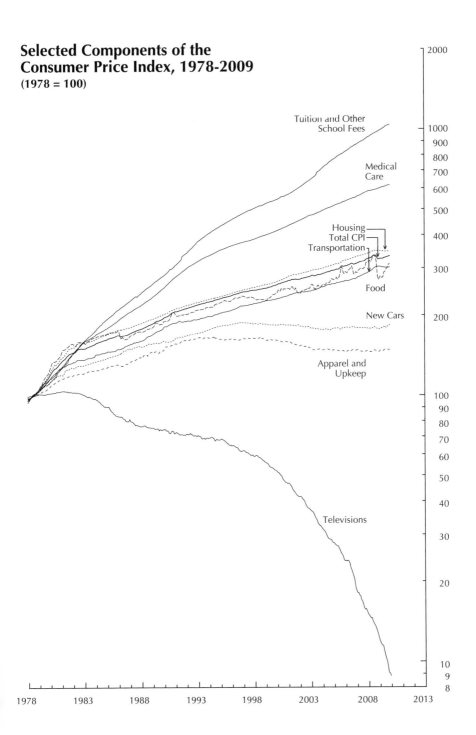

Output, Productivity,
and Distribution

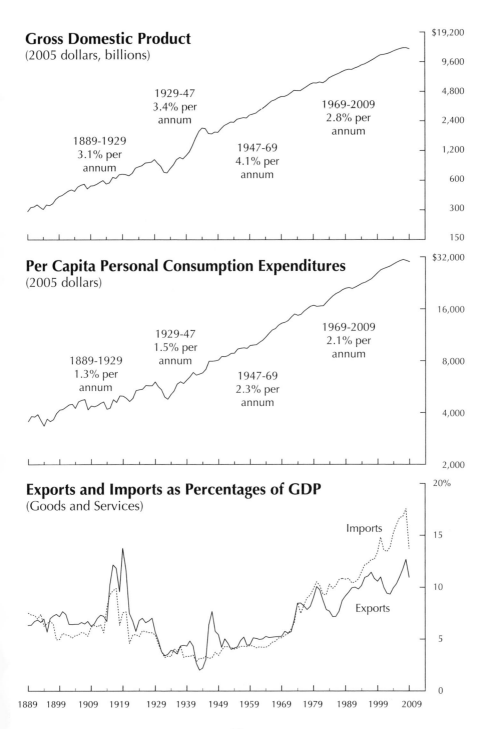

Gross Domestic Product
(2005 dollars, billions)

1889-1929
3.1% per
annum

1929-47
3.4% per
annum

1947-69
4.1% per
annum

1969-2009
2.8% per
annum

$19,200

9,600

4,800

2,400

1,200

600

300

150

Per Capita Personal Consumption Expenditures
(2005 dollars)

1889-1929
1.3% per
annum

1929-47
1.5% per
annum

1947-69
2.3% per
annum

1969-2009
2.1% per
annum

$32,000

16,000

8,000

4,000

2,000

Exports and Imports as Percentages of GDP
(Goods and Services)

Imports

Exports

20%

15

10

5

0

1889 1899 1909 1919 1929 1939 1949 1959 1969 1979 1989 1999 2009

17

U.S. Trading Partners, 2009
(Goods Only)

Exports
Total $1,287 Billion

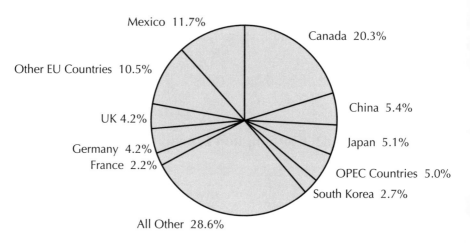

Mexico 11.7%

Canada 20.3%

Other EU Countries 10.5%

China 5.4%

UK 4.2%

Japan 5.1%

Germany 4.2%

OPEC Countries 5.0%

France 2.2%

South Korea 2.7%

All Other 28.6%

Imports
Total $2,104 Billion

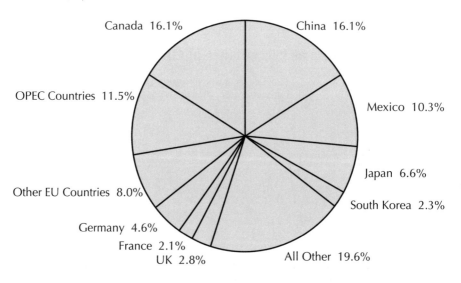

Canada 16.1%

China 16.1%

OPEC Countries 11.5%

Mexico 10.3%

Japan 6.6%

Other EU Countries 8.0%

South Korea 2.3%

Germany 4.6%

France 2.1%

UK 2.8%

All Other 19.6%

Index of Industrial Production
(2002=100)

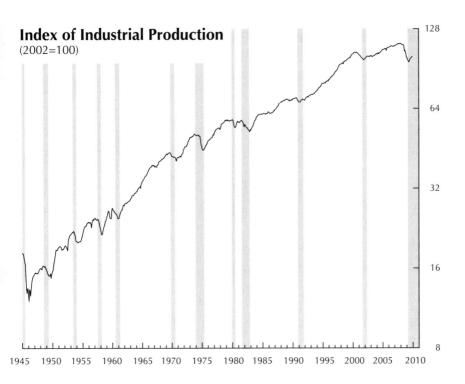

Capacity Utilization
(Percent of Capacity)

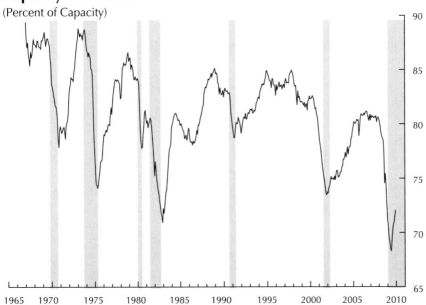

Value of New Construction Put in Place
(Seasonally Adjusted Annual Rates, Billions of 2006 Dollars)

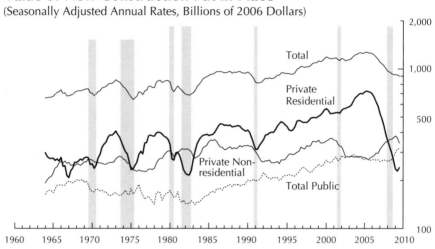

Characteristics of New Single-Family Homes

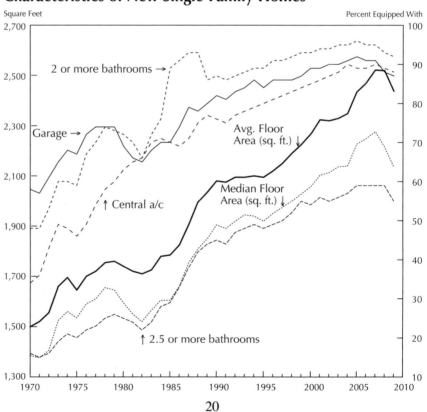

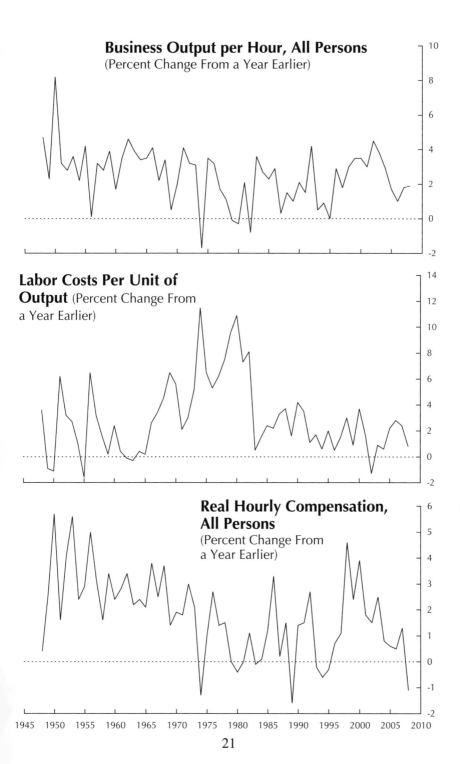

Business Output per Hour, All Persons
(Percent Change From a Year Earlier)

Labor Costs Per Unit of Output (Percent Change From a Year Earlier)

Real Hourly Compensation, All Persons
(Percent Change From a Year Earlier)

1945 1950 1955 1960 1965 1970 1975 1980 1985 1990 1995 2000 2005 2010

21

Economic Activity by Major Sector
(Billions of Chained 2005 Dollars)

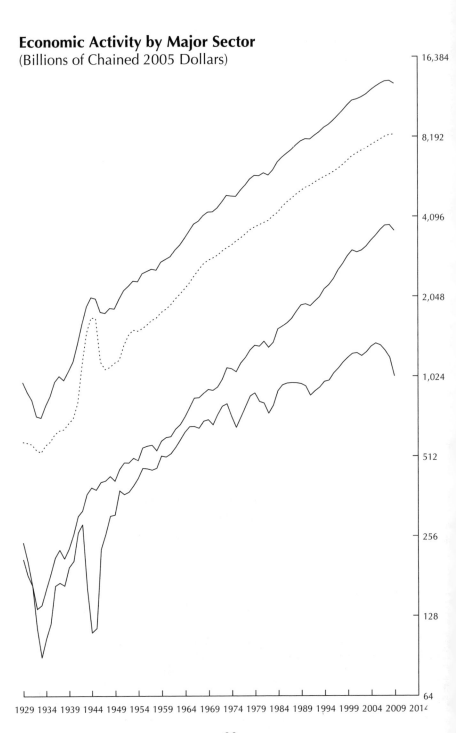

The Nation's Health Care Dollar, 2008

The U.S. spent $2.3 trillion on health care in 2008, or 16.2 percent of GDP.

Where It Came From

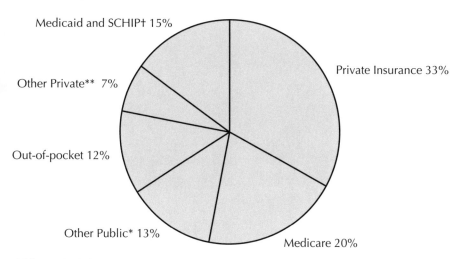

Medicaid and SCHIP† 15%

Other Private** 7%

Out-of-pocket 12%

Other Public* 13%

Private Insurance 33%

Medicare 20%

Where It Went

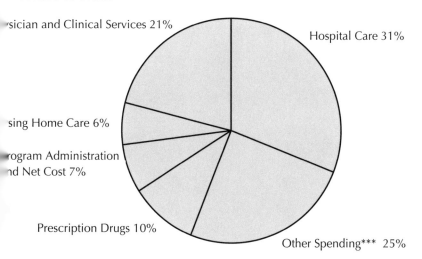

'sician and Clinical Services 21%

sing Home Care 6%

rogram Administration
nd Net Cost 7%

Prescription Drugs 10%

Hospital Care 31%

Other Spending*** 25%

† State Children's Health Insurance Program. * "Other public" includes programs such as workers' compensation, Department of Defense, Department of Veterans Affairs, Indian Health Service, and state and local hospital subsidies and school health. ** "Other private" includes industrial on-site care, privately funded construction, and non-patient revenues, including philanthropy. *** "Other spending" includes dentist services, other professional services, home health, durable medical products, over-the-counter medicines and sundries, public health, research and construction.

Population, Employment, and Income

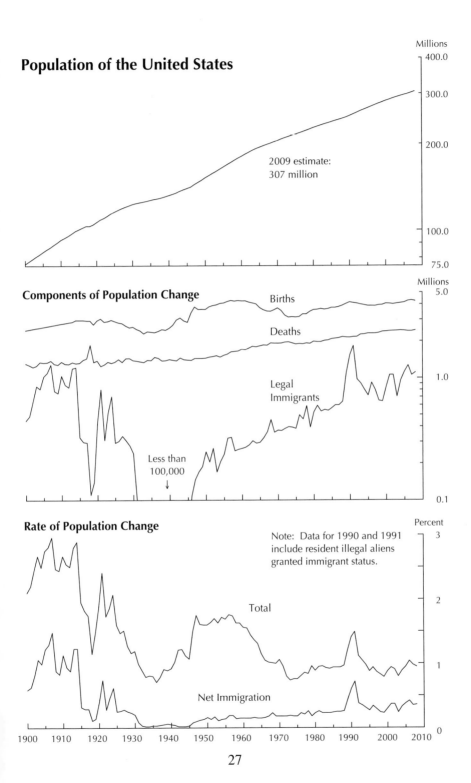

Population of the United States

Millions

400.0

300.0

200.0

2009 estimate:
307 million

100.0

75.0

Components of Population Change

Millions

5.0

Births

Deaths

1.0

Legal
Immigrants

Less than
100,000
↓

0.1

Rate of Population Change

Percent

Note: Data for 1990 and 1991
include resident illegal aliens
granted immigrant status.

3

2

Total

1

Net Immigration

0

1900   1910   1920   1930   1940   1950   1960   1970   1980   1990   2000   2010

U.S. Population and Labor Force, 1950 and 2000
(In millions, by sex and age)

Population and Labor Force, 1950

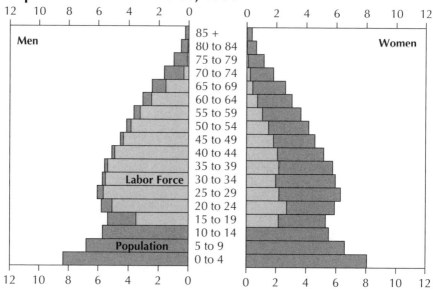

Population and Labor Force, 2000

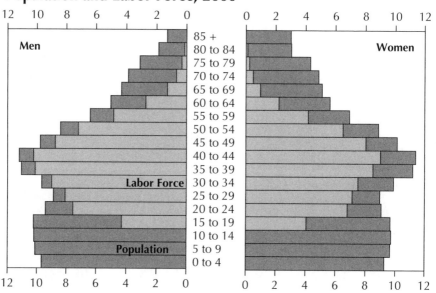

Employment by Selected Economic Sectors
(Thousands of Employees)

Manufacturing →

Retail Trade →

Health Care →

Financial Activities ↓

Wholesale Trade

Construction ↓

↑ Transportation & Warehousing

Mining & Natural Resources ↓

Education ↑

↑ Utilities

20,000

17,500

15,000

12,500

10,000

7,500

5,000

2,500

0

1939 1944 1949 1954 1959 1964 1969 1974 1979 1984 1989 1994 1999 2004 2009

29

Employed and Unemployed Persons*
(Millions of People)

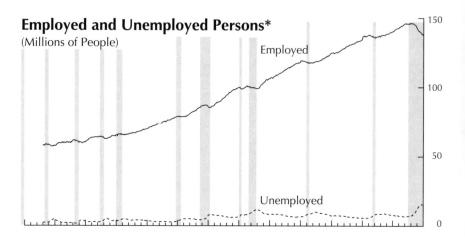

Unemployment as a Percent of the Civilian Labor Force

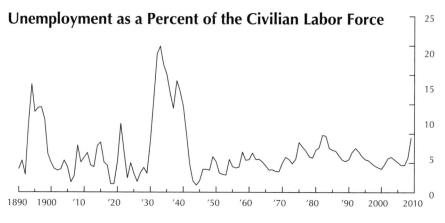

Reason for Unemployment
(Millions of People)

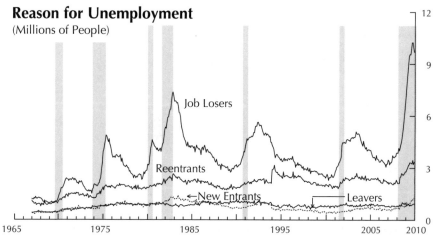

Nonagricultural Employees, by Major Sector
(Millions)

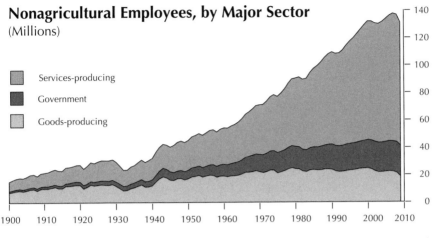

- Services-producing
- Government
- Goods-producing

Labor Force Participation Rates*

Labor Force as a
Percentage of Population

Employment as a
Percentage of Population

*Civilian Non-Institutional Population, Ages 16 and Older

Labor Force Participation Rates by Sex

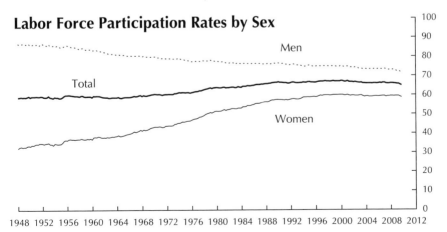

Men

Total

Women

Duration of Unemployment

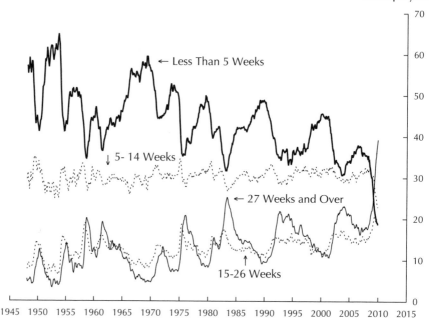

← Less Than 5 Weeks

↓ 5- 14 Weeks

← 27 Weeks and Over

↑ 15-26 Weeks

1945 1950 1955 1960 1965 1970 1975 1980 1985 1990 1995 2000 2005 2010 2015

The Median Income of Families
(By type of family, in constant 2008 dollars)

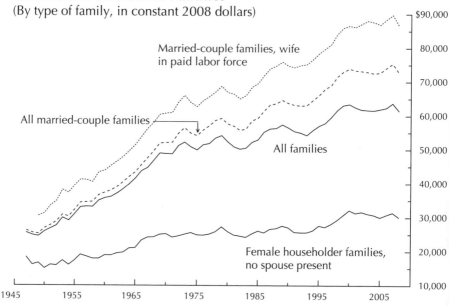

Married-couple families, wife
in paid labor force

All married-couple families

All families

Female householder families,
no spouse present

1945 1955 1965 1975 1985 1995 2005

32

Average Hourly Earnings for Production Workers
By Selected Economic Sectors (2009 Dollars)

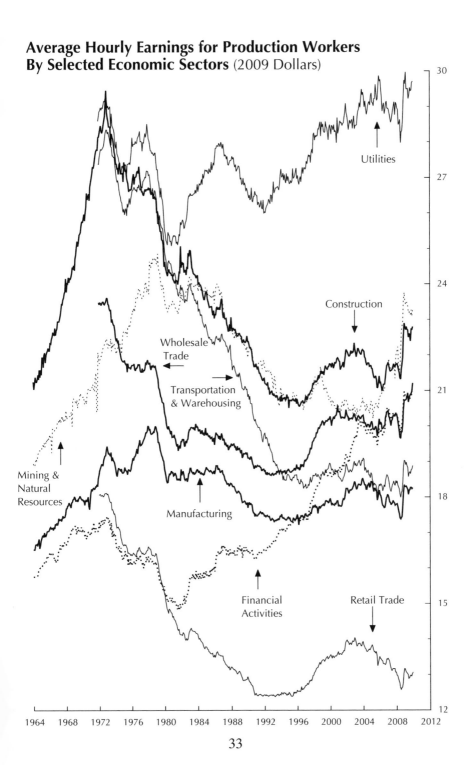

Government

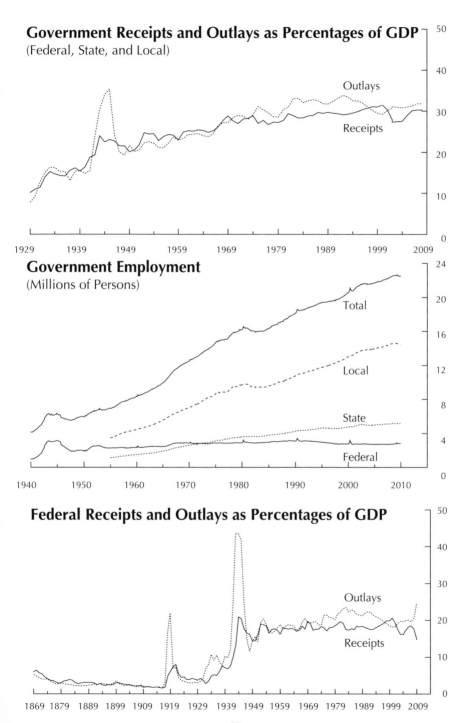

Government Receipts and Outlays as Percentages of GDP
(Federal, State, and Local)

Outlays

Receipts

50

40

30

20

10

0

1929   1939   1949   1959   1969   1979   1989   1999   2009

Government Employment
(Millions of Persons)

Total

Local

State

Federal

24

20

16

12

8

4

0

1940   1950   1960   1970   1980   1990   2000   2010

Federal Receipts and Outlays as Percentages of GDP

Outlays

Receipts

50

40

30

20

10

0

1869 1879 1889 1899 1909 1919 1929 1939 1949 1959 1969 1979 1989 1999 2009

37

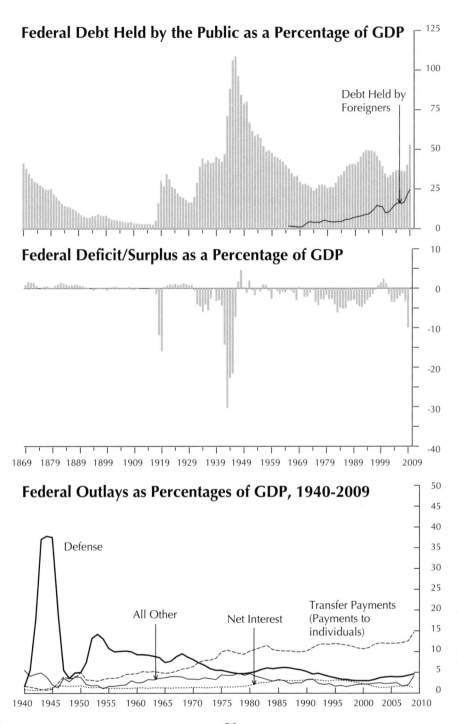

Federal Debt Held by the Public as a Percentage of GDP

Debt Held by Foreigners

Federal Deficit/Surplus as a Percentage of GDP

1869 1879 1889 1899 1909 1919 1929 1939 1949 1959 1969 1979 1989 1999 2009

Federal Outlays as Percentages of GDP, 1940-2009

Defense

All Other

Net Interest

Transfer Payments
(Payments to
individuals)

1940 1945 1950 1955 1960 1965 1970 1975 1980 1985 1990 1995 2000 2005 2010

38

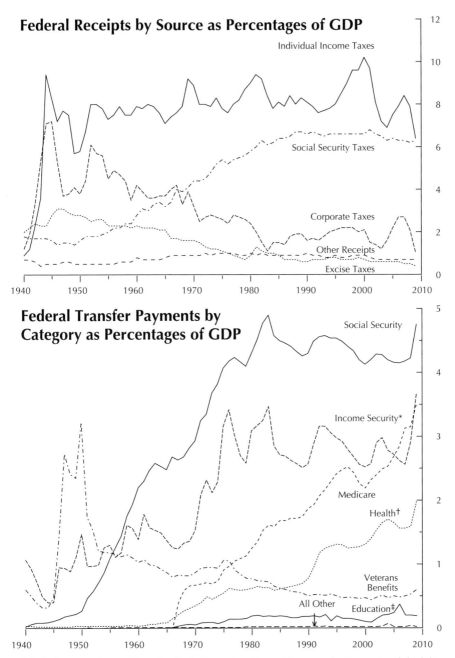

Federal Receipts by Source as Percentages of GDP

Individual Income Taxes

Social Security Taxes

Corporate Taxes

Other Receipts

Excise Taxes

Federal Transfer Payments by Category as Percentages of GDP

Social Security

Income Security*

Medicare

Health†

Veterans Benefits

All Other

Education‡

* Includes unemployment benefits, food stamps, housing assistance, and retirement and disability payments to Federal employees.
† Includes the Federal portion of Medicaid.
‡ Includes training, employment, and social services.

Capital Gains Taxes

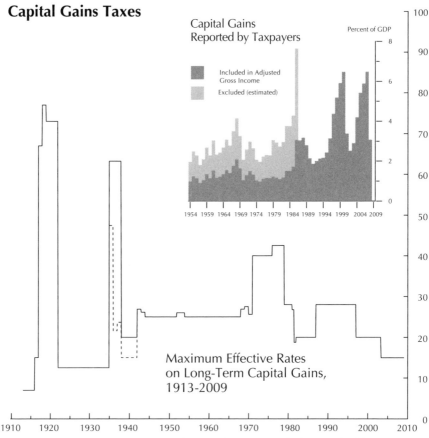

Capital Gains
Reported by Taxpayers

Percent of GDP

Included in Adjusted Gross Income

Excluded (estimated)

1954 1959 1964 1969 1974 1979 1984 1989 1994 1999 2004 2009

Maximum Effective Rates
on Long-Term Capital Gains,
1913-2009

1910   1920   1930   1940   1950   1960   1970   1980   1990   2000   2010

Prior to 1922 and for 1988-1990, the rates shown are the highest applicable to ordinary income. For other years the effective rate was lower, either because a portion of long-term gains was excluded from taxable income (the excludable portion was deemed a "tax preference" subject to the alternative minimum tax during the years 1971-1979), because the maximum tax on such gains was "capped" at a rate below that on ordinary income, or both.

The minimum holding period to qualify for a long-term gain has varied over the years. Currently it is one year. From 1922 through 1935 it was two years. During 1935-37, and from 1977 to 1985 it was one year. From 1938 through 1942 it was 18 months. From 1943 through 1976 and in 1986 and 1987 it was 6 months. During the years 1935 through 1941, larger reductions from ordinary income tax rates were granted on holding periods greater than the minimum, with the lowest rates (plotted as the dashed curve for those years) on assets held as long as 10 years.

Prior to 1987, the maximum effective tax rate on long-term gains applied to relatively few taxpayers with very high incomes — most taxpayers faced a lower rate. Since 1987, the maximum rate on long-term gains has applied to a much larger proportion of taxpayers. The current top rate is generally 15 percent for taxpayers whose regular tax bracket exceeds 15 percent.

Share of Income Taxes Paid By "The Rich"

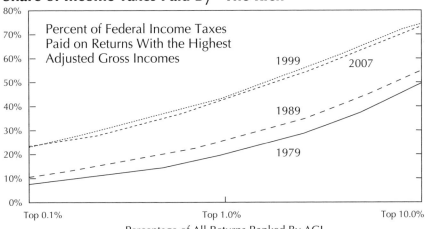

Percent of Federal Income Taxes Paid on Returns With the Highest Adjusted Gross Incomes

1999
2007
1989
1979

80%
70%
60%
50%
40%
30%
20%
10%
0%

Top 0.1%   Top 1.0%   Top 10.0%

Percentage of All Returns Ranked By AGI

Non-Withheld Individual Income Taxes as a Percent of the Total (Based on Totals Over 12-Month Spans)

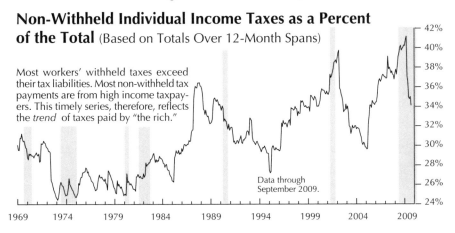

Most workers' withheld taxes exceed their tax liabilities. Most non-withheld tax payments are from high income taxpayers. This timely series, therefore, reflects the *trend* of taxes paid by "the rich."

Data through September 2009.

42%
40%
38%
36%
34%
32%
30%
28%
26%
24%

1969   1974   1979   1984   1989   1994   1999   2004   2009

Average Number of Days Spent Working Each Year to Pay Taxes

Includes individual income taxes, social insurance taxes, sales and excise taxes, property taxes, corporate income taxes, other business taxes, and all other taxes.

140
120
100
80
60
40
20
0

1900   1910   1920   1930   1940   1950   1960   1970   1980   1990   2000   2010

41

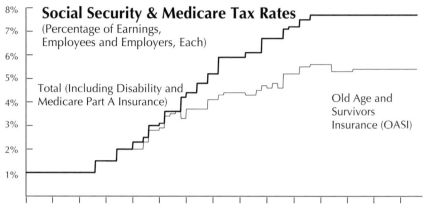

Social Security & Medicare Tax Rates
(Percentage of Earnings,
Employees and Employers, Each)

Total (Including Disability and
Medicare Part A Insurance)

Old Age and
Survivors
Insurance (OASI)

8%
7%
6%
5%
4%
3%
2%
1%

1937 1942 1947 1952 1957 1962 1967 1972 1977 1982 1987 1992 1997 2002 2007

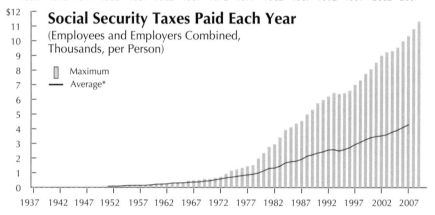

Social Security Taxes Paid Each Year
(Employees and Employers Combined,
Thousands, per Person)

▯ Maximum
— Average*

$12
11
10
9
8
7
6
5
4
3
2
1
0

1937 1942 1947 1952 1957 1962 1967 1972 1977 1982 1987 1992 1997 2002 2007

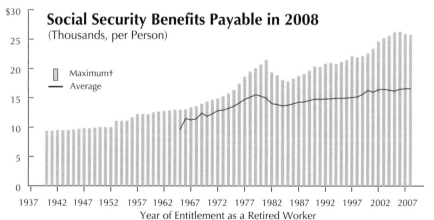

Social Security Benefits Payable in 2008
(Thousands, per Person)

▯ Maximum†
— Average

$30
25
20
15
10
5
0

1937 1942 1947 1952 1957 1962 1967 1972 1977 1982 1987 1992 1997 2002 2007
Year of Entitlement as a Retired Worker

* Paid by workers earning the national average wage.
† To workers who always earned the maximum taxable earnings prior to retirement at age 65. Does
not include spousal or dependent benefits.

42

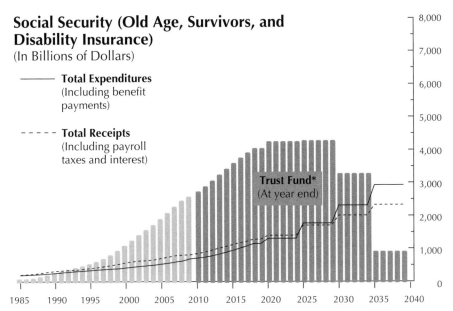

Social Security (Old Age, Survivors, and Disability Insurance)
(In Billions of Dollars)

——— **Total Expenditures**
(Including benefit payments)

- - - - - **Total Receipts**
(Including payroll taxes and interest)

Trust Fund*
(At year end)

Note: Data after 2009 are projections based on intermediate assumptions of economic and demographic trends. After 2019, projections are for five-year periods.

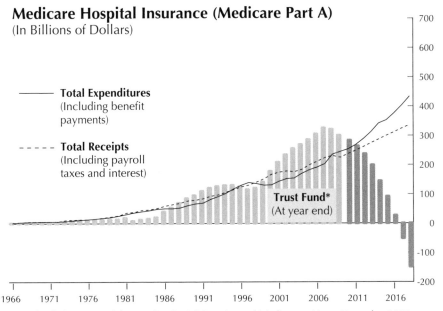

Medicare Hospital Insurance (Medicare Part A)
(In Billions of Dollars)

——— **Total Expenditures**
(Including benefit payments)

- - - - - **Total Receipts**
(Including payroll taxes and interest)

Trust Fund*
(At year end)

* Unfunded Treasury debt owed to Social Security and Medicare.   Note: Data after 2009 are projections based on intermediate assumptions of economic and demographic trends.

43

U.S. Economic and Military Assistance to the World
(1982-84 U.S. Dollars, Billions)

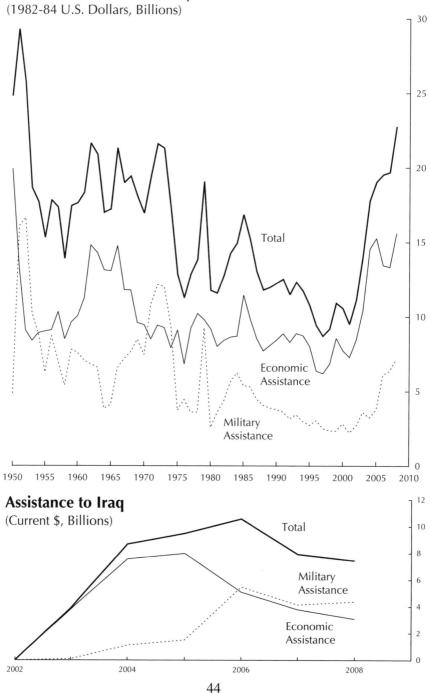

Assistance to Iraq
(Current $, Billions)

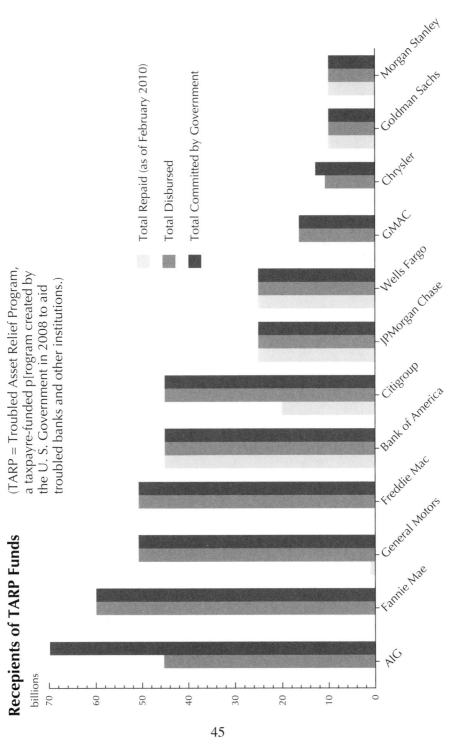

Recepients of TARP Funds

(TARP = Troubled Asset Relief Program, a taxpayre-funded p|rogram created by the U. S. Government in 2008 to aid troubled banks and other institutions.)

Total Repaid (as of February 2010)

Total Disbursed

Total Committed by Government

billions

Financial Indicators

Dollars of Debt per Dollar of GDP

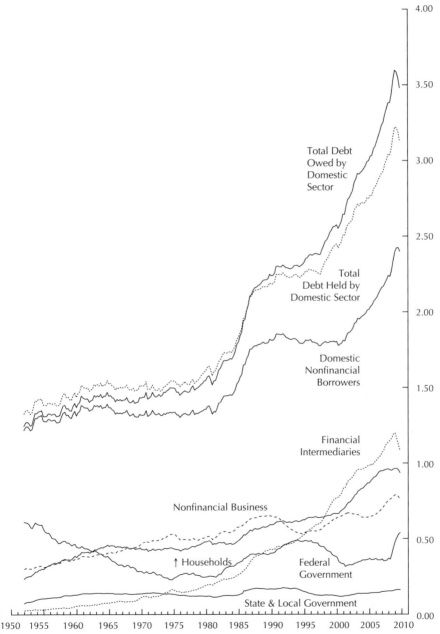

Note: The difference between the debt owed and the debt held by domestic sector is due to (or from) foreigners.

49

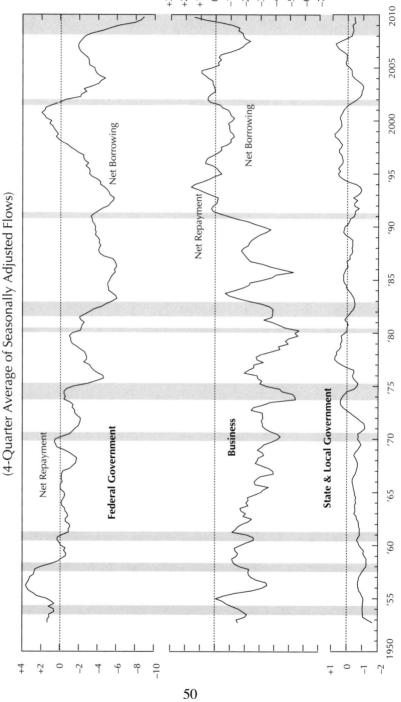

Sector Financial Flows as Percentages of GDP
(4-Quarter Average of Seasonally Adjusted Flows)

Net Repayment

Net Borrowing

Federal Government

Net Repayment

Net Borrowing

Business

State & Local Government

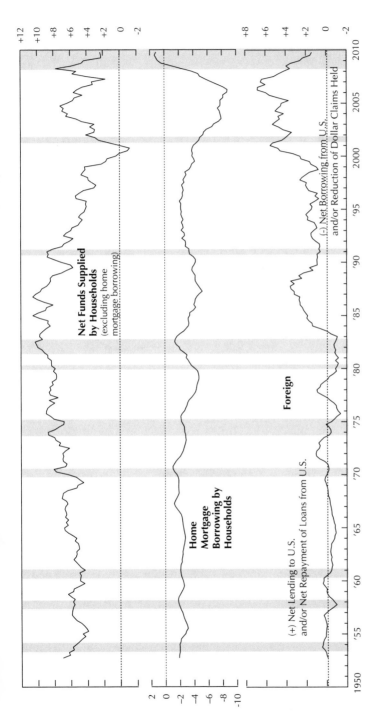

Net Funds Supplied by Households (excluding home mortgage borrowing)

Home Mortgage Borrowing by Households

Foreign

(+) Net Lending to U.S. and/or Net Repayment of Loans from U.S.

(-) Net Borrowing from U.S. and/or Reduction of Dollar Claims Held

Note: The data are based on the net change in financial assets less the net change in financial liabilities for each sector. For 2009 each percentage point represents about $144.6 billion. Shaded areas indicate recessionary periods. Latest data, 2009 fourth quarter.

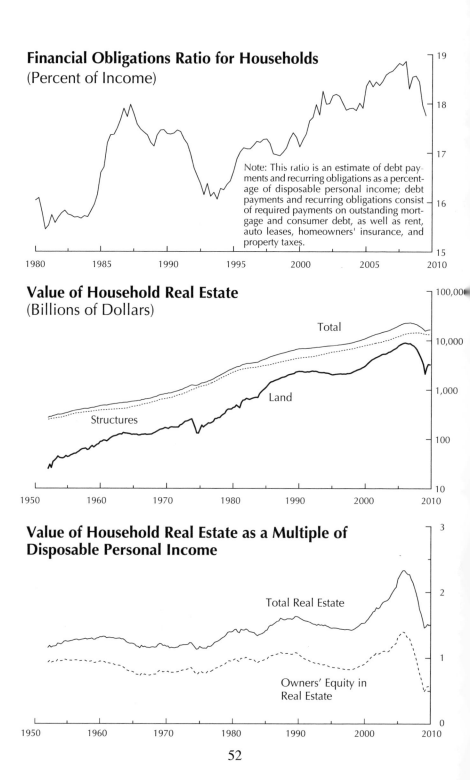

Financial Obligations Ratio for Households
(Percent of Income)

Note: This ratio is an estimate of debt payments and recurring obligations as a percentage of disposable personal income; debt payments and recurring obligations consist of required payments on outstanding mortgage and consumer debt, as well as rent, auto leases, homeowners' insurance, and property taxes.

1980   1985   1990   1995   2000   2005   2010

19
18
17
16
15

Value of Household Real Estate
(Billions of Dollars)

Total

Land

Structures

1950   1960   1970   1980   1990   2000   2010

100,00
10,000
1,000
100
10

Value of Household Real Estate as a Multiple of
Disposable Personal Income

Total Real Estate

Owners' Equity in
Real Estate

1950   1960   1970   1980   1990   2000   2010

3
2
1
0

52

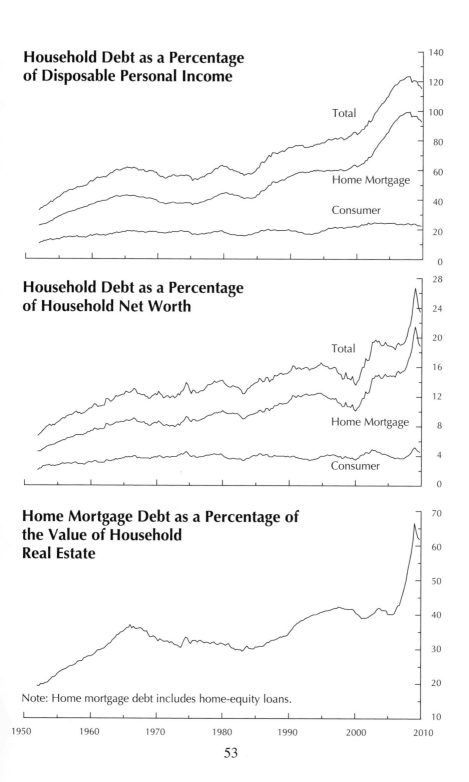

Household Debt as a Percentage of Disposable Personal Income

Total

Home Mortgage

Consumer

140
120
100
80
60
40
20
0

Household Debt as a Percentage of Household Net Worth

Total

Home Mortgage

Consumer

28
24
20
16
12
8
4
0

Home Mortgage Debt as a Percentage of the Value of Household Real Estate

Note: Home mortgage debt includes home-equity loans.

70
60
50
40
30
20
10

1950   1960   1970   1980   1990   2000   2010

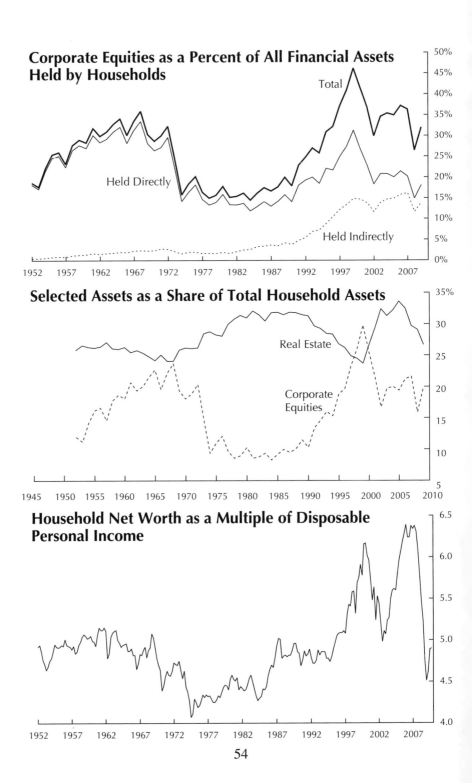

Corporate Equities as a Percent of All Financial Assets Held by Households

Total

Held Directly

Held Indirectly

50%
45%
40%
35%
30%
25%
20%
15%
10%
5%
0%

1952   1957   1962   1967   1972   1977   1982   1987   1992   1997   2002   2007

Selected Assets as a Share of Total Household Assets

Real Estate

Corporate Equities

35%
30
25
20
15
10
5

1945   1950   1955   1960   1965   1970   1975   1980   1985   1990   1995   2000   2005   2010

Household Net Worth as a Multiple of Disposable Personal Income

6.5
6.0
5.5
5.0
4.5
4.0

1952   1957   1962   1967   1972   1977   1982   1987   1992   1997   2002   2007

54

The Total Value of Corporate Stocks* and the Value of Stocks Held by Selected Sectors
(Billions of Dollars)

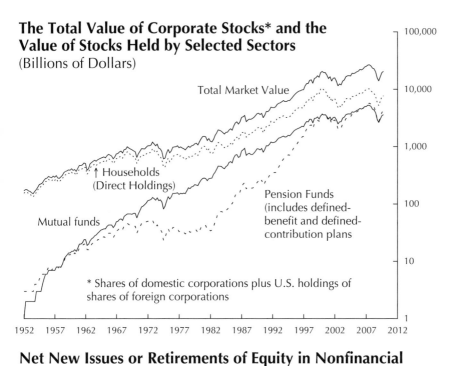

Total Market Value

Households (Direct Holdings)

Mutual funds

Pension Funds (includes defined-benefit and defined-contribution plans

100,000

10,000

1,000

100

10

1

* Shares of domestic corporations plus U.S. holdings of shares of foreign corporations

1952   1957   1962   1967   1972   1977   1982   1987   1992   1997   2002   2007   2012

Net New Issues or Retirements of Equity in Nonfinancial Corporate Business as a Percent of Market Value of Outstanding Equity at Start of Each Quarter
(Four-Quarter Moving Average)

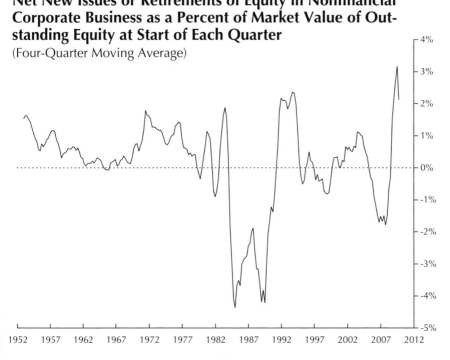

4%

3%

2%

1%

0%

-1%

-2%

-3%

-4%

-5%

1952   1957   1962   1967   1972   1977   1982   1987   1992   1997   2002   2007   2012

55

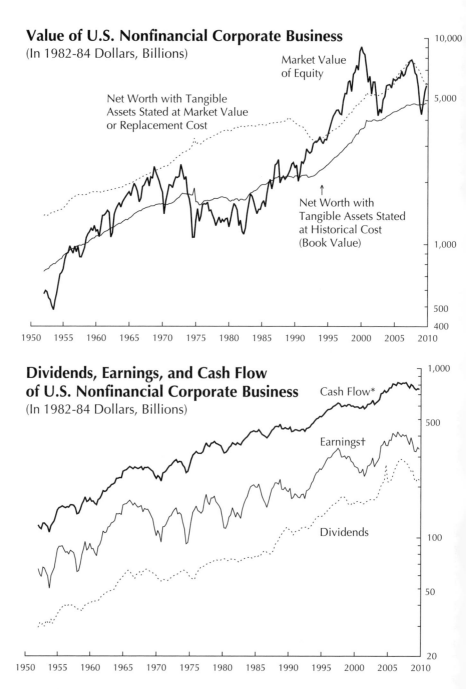

Value of U.S. Nonfinancial Corporate Business
(In 1982-84 Dollars, Billions)

Market Value of Equity

Net Worth with Tangible Assets Stated at Market Value or Replacement Cost

Net Worth with Tangible Assets Stated at Historical Cost (Book Value)

10,000

5,000

1,000

500

400

1950 1955 1960 1965 1970 1975 1980 1985 1990 1995 2000 2005 2010

Dividends, Earnings, and Cash Flow of U.S. Nonfinancial Corporate Business
(In 1982-84 Dollars, Billions)

Cash Flow*

Earnings†

Dividends

1,000

500

100

50

20

1950 1955 1960 1965 1970 1975 1980 1985 1990 1995 2000 2005 2010

* Includes inventory valuation adjustment.
† Includes capital consumption adjustment and retained earnings of foreign subsidiaries.

56

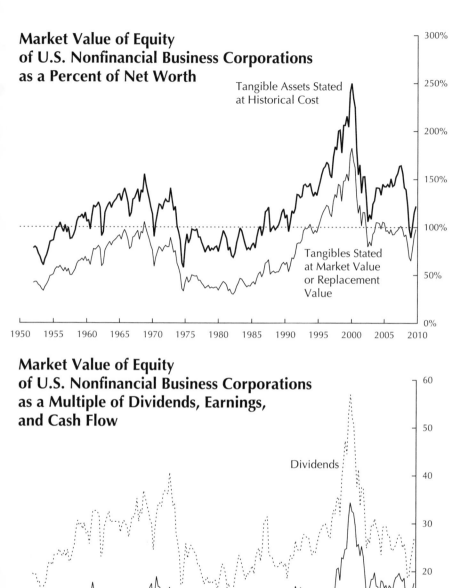

Market Value of Equity
of U.S. Nonfinancial Business Corporations
as a Percent of Net Worth

Tangible Assets Stated at Historical Cost

Tangibles Stated at Market Value or Replacement Value

300%
250%
200%
150%
100%
50%
0%

1950 1955 1960 1965 1970 1975 1980 1985 1990 1995 2000 2005 2010

Market Value of Equity
of U.S. Nonfinancial Business Corporations
as a Multiple of Dividends, Earnings, and Cash Flow

Dividends

Earnings†

Cash Flow*

60
50
40
30
20
10
0

1950 1955 1960 1965 1970 1975 1980 1985 1990 1995 2000 2005 2010

* Includes inventory valuation adjustment.
† Includes capital-consumption adjustment and retained earnings of foreign subsidiaries.

57

Dow Jones Industrials Average, Standard & Poor's Index of 500 Common Stock Prices, and the NASDAQ

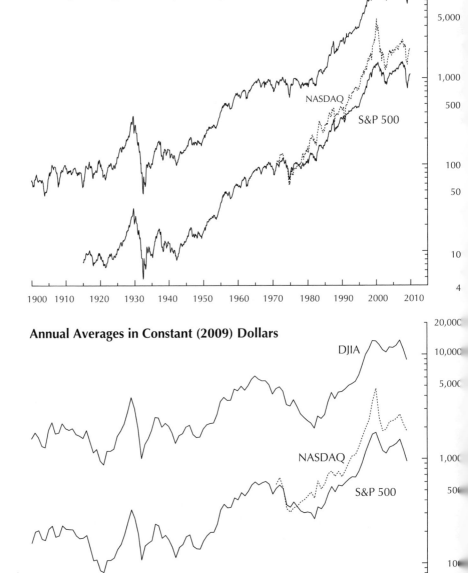

Monthly Averages of Daily Closings

DJIA

NASDAQ

S&P 500

20,000
10,000
5,000
1,000
500
100
50
10
4

1900 1910 1920 1930 1940 1950 1960 1970 1980 1990 2000 2010

Annual Averages in Constant (2009) Dollars

DJIA

NASDAQ

S&P 500

20,000
10,000
5,000
1,000
500
100
50

1900 1910 1920 1930 1940 1950 1960 1970 1980 1990 2000 2010

"Misery Index"
(Unemployment Rate Plus Inflation Rate)

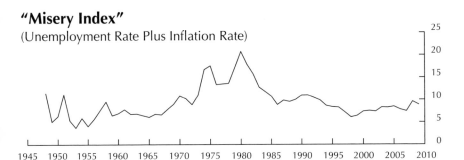

"Fear Index" (Chicago Board Options Exchange Volatility Index) and S&P 500

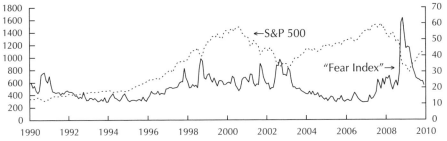

University of Michigan's Index of Consumer Sentiment

S&P/Case-Shiller U.S. National Home Price Index
(2000=100)

Energy

World Crude Oil Production
(Million Barrels per Day)

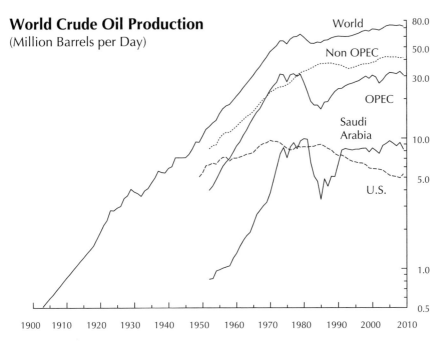

World ⌐ 80.0

Non OPEC ⌐ 50.0

⌐ 30.0

OPEC

Saudi
Arabia ⌐ 10.0

⌐ 5.0

U.S.

⌐ 1.0

⌐ 0.5

1900 1910 1920 1930 1940 1950 1960 1970 1980 1990 2000 2010

The Price of Crude Oil
(Constant-Dollar (2009) Price per Barrel*)

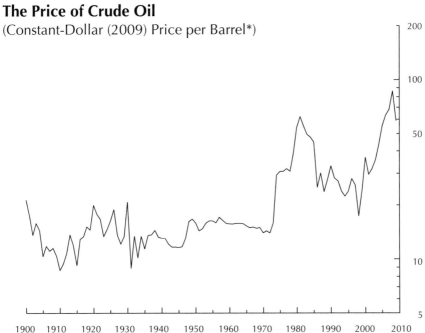

⌐ 200

⌐ 100

⌐ 50

⌐ 10

⌐ 5

1900 1910 1920 1930 1940 1950 1960 1970 1980 1990 2000 2010

* Based on the Wholesale Price Index for all commodities. Latest plot, 2009.

Gasoline Prices
(Dollars per Gallon, Including Taxes)

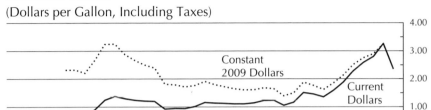

Heating Oil Prices
(Dollars per Gallon)

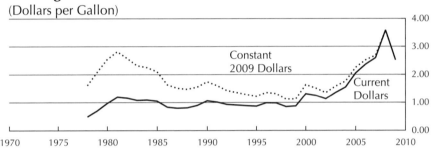

Natural Gas Prices
(Dollars per Thousand Cubic Feet)

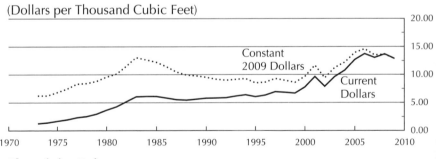

Electricity Prices
(Cents per Kilowatt-hour)

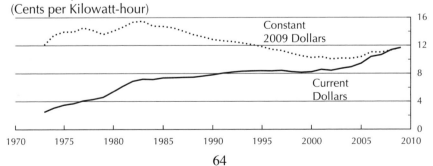

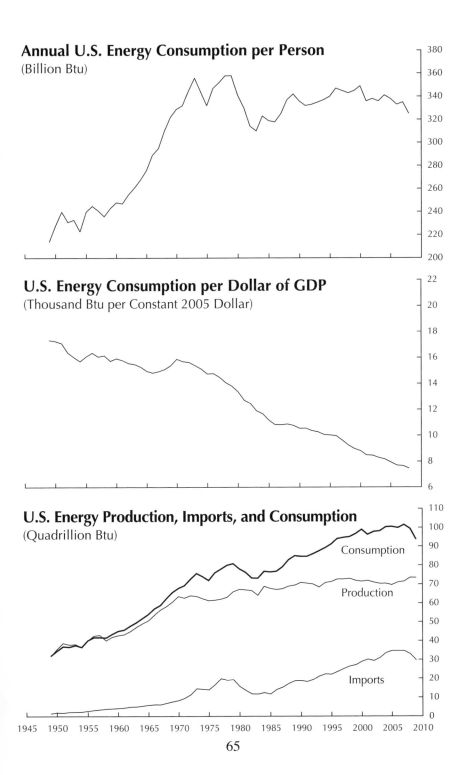

Annual U.S. Energy Consumption per Person
(Billion Btu)

380
360
340
320
300
280
260
240
220
200

U.S. Energy Consumption per Dollar of GDP
(Thousand Btu per Constant 2005 Dollar)

22
20
18
16
14
12
10
8
6

U.S. Energy Production, Imports, and Consumption
(Quadrillion Btu)

Consumption

Production

Imports

110
100
90
80
70
60
50
40
30
20
10
0

1945 1950 1955 1960 1965 1970 1975 1980 1985 1990 1995 2000 2005 2010

65

U.S. Energy Production by Source
(Quadrillion Btu)

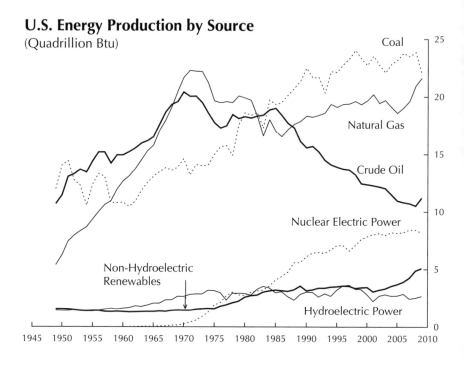

U.S. Energy Consumption by Source
(Quadrillion Btu)

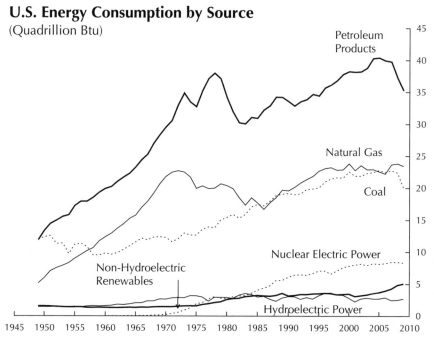

Energy Flow in the United States, 2008
(Quadrillion Btu)

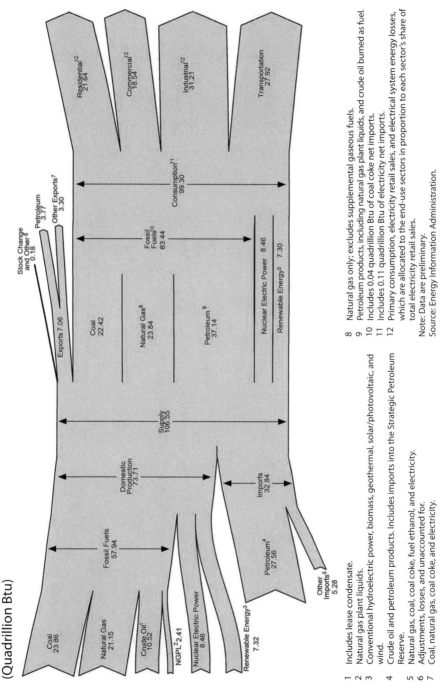

1 Includes lease condensate.
2 Natural gas plant liquids.
3 Conventional hydroelectric power, biomass, geothermal, solar/photovoltaic, and wind.
4 Crude oil and petroleum products. Includes imports into the Strategic Petroleum Reserve.
5 Natural gas, coal, coal coke, fuel ethanol, and electricity.
6 Adjustments, losses, and unaccounted for.
7 Coal, natural gas, coal coke, and electricity.

8 Natural gas only; excludes supplemental gaseous fuels.
9 Petroleum products, including natural gas plant liquids, and crude oil burned as fuel.
10 Includes 0.04 quadrillion Btu of coal coke net imports.
11 Includes 0.11 quadrillion Btu of electricity net imports.
12 Primary consumption, electricity retail sales, and electrical system energy losses, which are allocated to the end-use sectors in proportion to each sector's share of total electricity retail sales.

Note: Data are preliminary.
Source: Energy Information Administration.

U.S. Primary Energy Consumption by Source and Sector, 2008
(Quadrillion Btu)

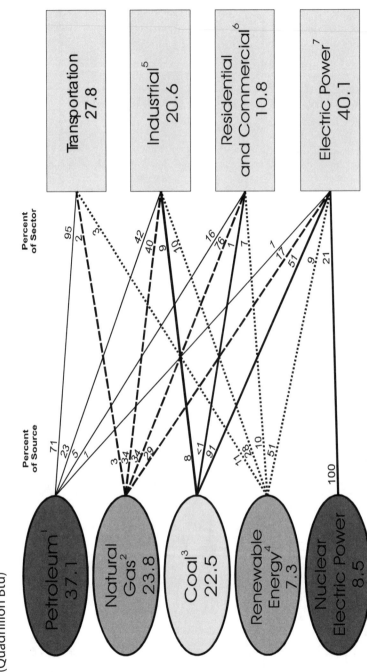

1 Does not include the fuel ethanol portion of motor gasoline—fuel ethanol is included in "Renewable Energy."
2 Excludes supplemental gaseous fuels.
3 Includes less than 0.1 quadrillion Btu of coal coke net imports.
4 Conventional hydroelectric power, geothermal, solar/PV, wind, and biomass.

6 Includes commercial combined-heat-and-power (CHP) and commercial electricity-only plants.
7 Electricity-only and combined-heat-and-power (CHP) plants whose primary business is to sell electricity, or electricity and heat, to the public.

Note: Sum of components may not equal 100 percent due to independent rounding.

Sources of Data in Charts

Page	Source
3	B
4	B,E;B,E
5	B,E;B,E
6	E;E
7	D
8,9	B,G,H
10	B,H
11	B,E;B,E;B,E
12	B
13	B
17	A;A;A
18	A
19	D;D
20	T;T
21	B;B;B
22	A
23	C;C
27	E,I,Q;E,I,Q;E,I,Q
28	B
29	B
30	B;B;B
31	B;B;B
32	B;T
33	B
37	A;B;J
38	J;J;J
39	J;J
40	L
41	L;P;O
42	K;K;K
43	K;C
44	U;U
45	W
49	F
50,51	F
52	F;F;F
53	F;F;F
54	F;F;F
55	F;F

Page	Source
56	F;F
57	F;F
58	V;V
59	B
59	N;N;M
63	S;B;R;S
64	B,S;B,S;B,S;B,S;B,S
65	E,S;A,S;S
66	S;S
67	S
68	S

A. Bureau of Economic Analysis
B. Bureau of Labor Statistics
C. Centers for Medicare & Medicaid Services
D. Federal Reserve Board
E. Federal Reserve Bank of St. Louis
F. Federal Reserve *Flow of Funds Accounts*
G. International Monetary Fund
H. Kitco
I. National Vital Statistics Report
J. Office of Management and Budget
K. Social Security Administration
L. IRS *Statistics of Income Bulletin*
M. Standard & Poor's
N. Survey Research Center, University of Michigan
O. Tax Foundation
P. *Treasury Bulletin*
Q. U.S. Department of Homeland Security
R. U.S. Department of Energy
S. U.S. Energy Information Administration
T. U.S. Census bureau
U. USAID
V. Yahoo! Finance
W. Propublica

The Benefits of
AIER MEMBERSHIP

If you found this book helpful, you'll also benefit from AIER's newsletters. Our timely articles offer valuable insight on important economic and personal finance issues.

Our twice-monthly *Research Reports* provide concise discussion concerning a wide range of current issues. One article each month is devoted to deciphering where we are in the business cycle.

Our monthly *Economic Bulletin* presents in-depth treatment of topics pertaining to economics, fiscal policy, retirement, and personal finance.

Once you become a member you will also receive 50% off all AIER books. Support our educational efforts by becoming an AIER member today. Print and digital memberships now available.

Call us toll-free: (888) 528-1216

Visit us online: www.aier.org